1A

T

PIANO · VOCAL · GUITAR

100 KiDS' SONGS

ISBN 0-634-01494-3

HAL•LEONARD®
CORPORATION

7777 W. BLUEMOUND RD. P.O. BOX 13819 MILWAUKEE, WI 53213

Visit Hal Leonard Online at
www.halleonard.com

784.624 ONE

100 KIDS' SONGS

A-HUNTING WE WILL GO

Traditional

A-TISKET A-TASKET

Traditional

ALL NIGHT, ALL DAY

Spiritual

ALPHABET SONG

Traditional

A B C D E F G H I J K L M N O P

Q R S and T U V W (dou - ble - U) and X Y Z.

Now you've heard my A B C; Tell me what you think of me.

ALOUETTE

Traditional

Je te plu - me - rai la têt'; je te plu - me - rai la tet'.

no chord **Repeat as needed *** **D.C. al Fine**

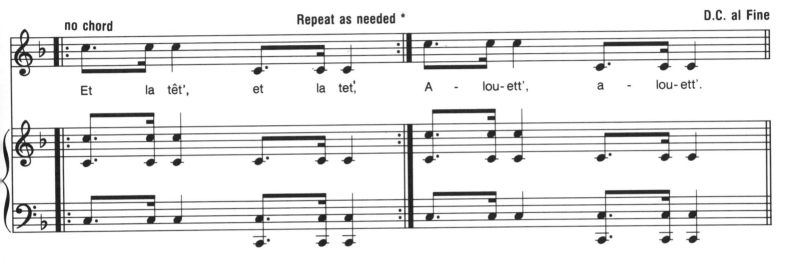

Et la têt', et la tet', A - lou-ett', a - lou-ett'.

*Each chorus adds a new part of the body, in reverse order. For example, Chorus 3 is sung:

> Et le nez, et le nez,
> Et le bec, et le bec,
> Et la têt', et le têt',
> Alouett', Alouett'.
> Oh, *etc.*

2. le bec *(beak)*
3. le nez *(nose)*
4. les yeux *(eyes)*
5. le cou *(neck)*

6. les ailes *(wings)*
7. le dos *(back)*
8. les pattes *(feet)*
9. la queue *(tail)*

AMERICA
(My Country 'Tis of Thee)

Words by SAMUEL FRANCIS SMITH
Traditional Music

1. My coun - try 'tis of thee,
2. My na - tive coun - try, thee,
3.-4. *See additional lyrics*

sweet land of lib - er - ty of thee I
land of of the no - ble free, of thy name I

sing.
love.

Land where my fa - thers died!
I where love thy rocks and rills,

Additional Lyrics

3. Let music swell the breeze
   And ring from all the trees
   Sweet freedom's song.
   Let mortal tongues awake;
   Let all that breathe partake;
   Let rocks their silence break,
   The sound prolong.

4. Our fathers's God, to Thee
   Author of liberty,
   To Thee we sing.
   Long may our land be bright
   With freedom's holy light;
   Protect us by Thy might,
   Great God, our King!

AMERICA THE BEAUTIFUL

Words by KATHERINE LEE BATES
Music by SAMUEL A. WARD

2. O beautiful for pilgrim feet,
   Whose stern impassioned stress,
   A thoroughfare for freedom beat
   Across the wilderness.
   America! America!
   God mend thine ev'ry flaw,
   Confirm thy soul in self-control,
   Thy liberty in law.

3. O beautiful for patriot dream
   That sees beyond the years,
   Thine alabaster cities gleam,
   Undimmed by human tears.
   America! America!
   God shed His grace on thee,
   And crown thy good with brotherhood
   From sea to shining sea.

ANIMAL FAIR

American Folksong

BAA BAA BLACK SHEEP

Traditional

BE KIND TO YOUR WEB-FOOTED FRIENDS

Traditional

March

Be kind to your web-foot-ed friends, _____ for a

duck may be some-bod-y's moth - er. You

may think that this is the end, _____ and it is.

BARNYARD SONG

Traditional

*Note: On each verse repeat chorus for all previous verses

Additional lyrics:

I had a pig and the pig pleased me.
I fed my pig on a green berry tree.
The little pig went "oink oink"
Chorus:

I had a cow and the cow pleased me.
I fed my cow on a green berry tree.
The little cow went "moo moo"
Chorus:

I had a baby and the baby pleased me.
I fed my baby on a green berry tree.
The little baby went "waah waah"
Chorus:

THE BEAR WENT OVER THE MOUNTAIN

Traditional

Oh, the bear went o-ver the

moun - tain, the bear went o - ver the moun - tain, the bear went o - ver the

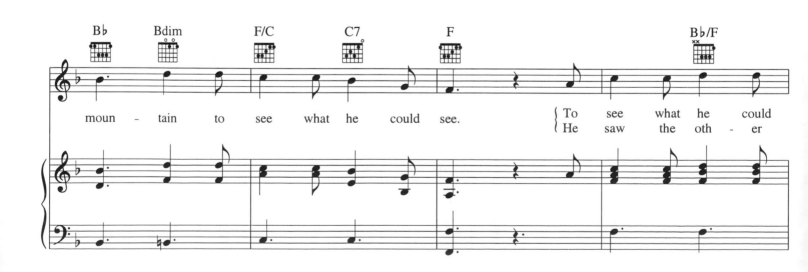

moun - tain to see what he could see. To see what he could
He saw the oth - er

BINGO

NOTE: Each time a letter of BINGO is deleted
in the lyric, clap your hands in place of singing
the letter.

Traditional

THE BLUE TAIL FLY
(Jimmy Crack Corn)

Words and Music by
DANIEL DECATUR EMMETT

BYE, BABY BUNTING

Traditional

Gently

Bye bye ba - by bunt - ing, dad - dy's gone a hunt - ing, to

get a lit - tle rab - bit skin to

wrap the ba - by bunt - ing in.

DOWN IN MY HEART

Traditional

(Oh, My Darling)
CLEMENTINE

Words and Music by
PERCY MONTROSE

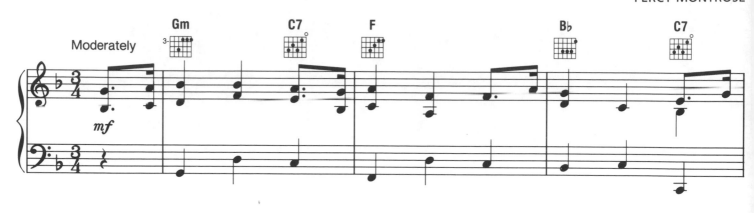

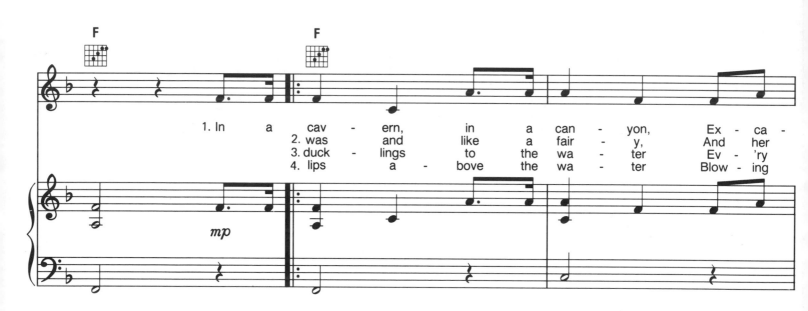

1. In a cav - ern, in a can - yon, Ex - ca -
2. was and like a fair - y, And her
3. duck - lings to the wa - ter Ev - 'ry
4. lips a - bove the wa - ter Blow - ing

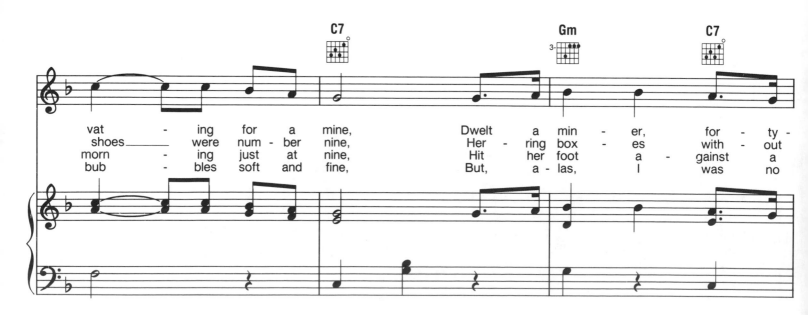

vat - ing for a mine, Dwelt a min - er, for - ty
shoes_____ were num - ber nine, Her - ring box - es with - out
morn - ing just at nine, Hit her foot a - gainst a
bub - bles soft and fine, But, a - las, I was no

COCK-A-DOODLE-DOO

Traditional

Happily

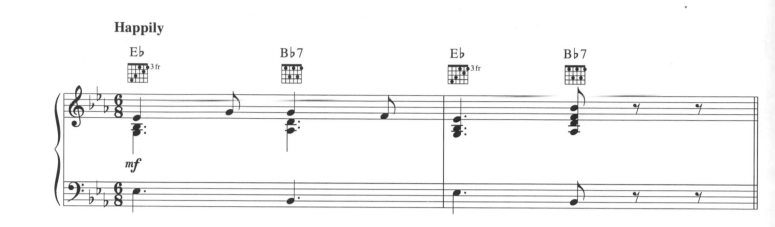

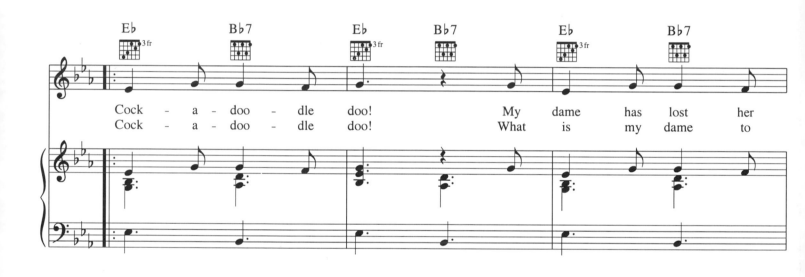

Cock - a - doo - dle doo! My dame has lost her
Cock - a - doo - dle doo! What is my dame to

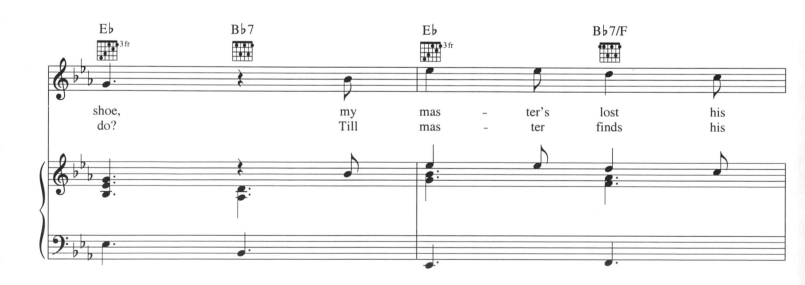

shoe, my mas - ter's lost his
do? Till mas - ter finds his

DO YOUR EARS HANG LOW?

Traditional

Do your (D.S.) ears hang low? Do they
Can your ears stand high? Can they

DOWN BY THE STATION

Traditional

Down by the sta - tion

ear - ly in the morn - ing, see the lit - tle

puf - fer - bil - lies all in a

DRY BONES

Traditional

Moderately

E - ze - kiel cried, "Them dry bones!" E -
ze - kiel cried, "Them dry bones!" E - ze - kiel cried, "Them
dry bones!" Oh hear the word of the Lord! The

EENSY WEENSY SPIDER

Traditional

Playfully, in 2

The een-sy ween-sy spi - der went up the wa - ter spout; Down came the

rain and washed the spi - der out. Out came the sun and dried up all the

rain; Now the een-sy ween-sy spi - der went up the spout a - gain.

THE FARMER IN THE DELL

Traditional

3. The wife takes a child, etc.

4. The child takes a nurse, etc.

5. The nurse takes a dog, etc.

6. The dog takes a cat, etc.

7. The cat takes a rat, etc.

8. The rat takes the cheese, etc.

9. The cheese stands alone, etc.

EVENING PRAYER

from HANSEL AND GRETEL

By ENGELBERT HUMPERDINCK

FOR HE'S A JOLLY GOOD FELLOW

Traditional

FRERE JACQUES
(Are You Sleeping?)

Traditional

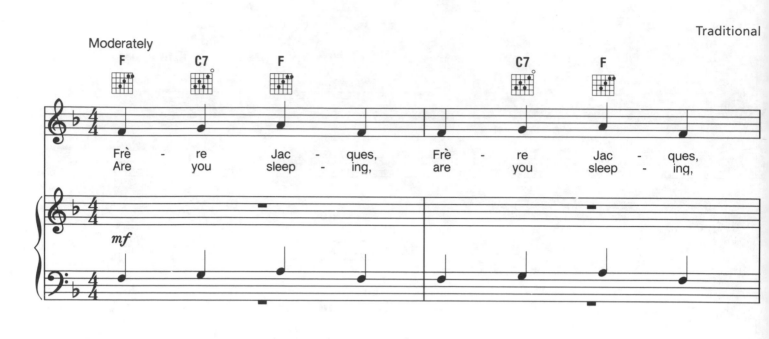

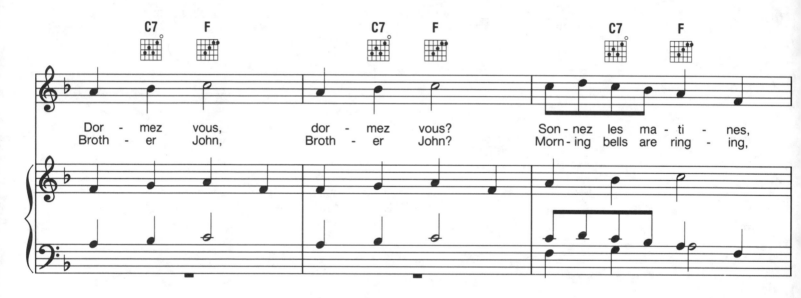

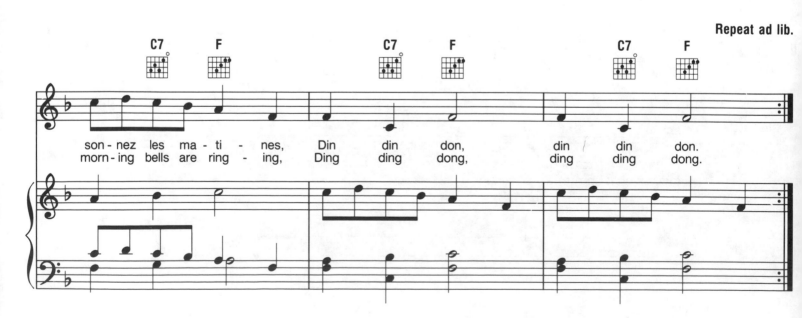

GIT ALONG, LITTLE DOGIES

Western American Cowboy Song

As I was a- walk- ing one
Ear- ly in spring we round
Whoop- ing and yell- ing round and

morn- ing for pleas- ure I saw a cow- punch- er come
up all for the dog- ies. We mark 'em and brand 'em and
round- ing the dog- ies from sun- rise till sun- set and

FROG WENT A-COURTIN'

Traditional

Additional Lyrics

2. Well, he rode down to Miss Mouses's door, uh-huh, uh-huh.
   Well, he rode down to Miss Mouses's door,
   Where he had often been before, uh-huh, uh-huh.

3. He took Miss Mousie on his knee, uh-huh, uh-huh.
   He took Miss Mousie on his knee,
   Said, "Miss Mousie will you marry me?" Uh-huh, uh-huh.

4. "I'll have to ask my Uncle Rat, etc.
   See what he will say to that." etc.

5. "Without my Uncle Rat's consent,
   I would not marry the President."

6. Well, Uncle Rat laughed and shook his fat sides,
   To think his niece would be a bride.

7. Well, Uncle Rat rode off to town
   To buy his niece a wedding gown.

8. "Where will the wedding supper be?"
   "Way down yonder in a hollow tree."

9. "What will wedding supper be?"
   "A fried mosquito and a roasted flea."

10. First to come in were two little ants,
    Fixing around to have a dance.

11. Next to come in was a bumble bee,
    Bouncing a fiddle on his knee.

12. Next to come in was a fat sassy lad,
    Thinks himself as big as his dad.

13. Thinks himself a man indeed,
    Because he chews the tobacco weed.

14. And next to come in was a big tomcat,
    He swallowed the frog and the mouse and the rat.

15. Next to come in was a big old snake,
    He chased the party into the lake.

GO TELL AUNT RHODY

Traditional

1. Go tell Aunt Rho - dy,
2.-5. *(See additional lyrics)*

Additional Lyrics

2. **The one she was saving,** *(three times)*
   To make a feather bed.

3. **The gander is weeping,** *(three times)*
   Because his wife is dead.

4. **The goslings are crying,** *(three times)*
   Because their mama's dead.

5. **She died in the water,** *(three times)*
   With her heels above her head.

GOOBER PEAS

Words by P. PINDAR
Music by P. NUTT

GOOSEY, GOOSEY GANDER

Traditional

HE'S GOT THE WHOLE WORLD IN HIS HANDS

African-American Folksong

GRANDFATHER'S CLOCK

By HENRY CLAY WORK

old man_____ died. Nine-ty years with-out slum-ber-ing,

pp

tick, tock, tick, tock, His life sec-onds num-ber-ing, tick, tock, tick, tock. It

stopped short nev-er to go a-gain when the old man died.

In watching its pendulum swing to and fro,
Many hours had he spent while a boy;
And in childhood and manhood the
      clock seemed to know,
And to share both his grief and his joy.
For it struck twenty-four when he entered
      at the door,
With a blooming and beautiful bride.

My grandfather said that of those he could hire,
Not a servant so faithful he found;
For it wasted no time, and had but one desire,
At the close of each week to be wound.
And it kept in its place, not a frown upon its face,
And its hands never hung by its side.

It rang an alarm in the dead of the night,
An alarm that for years had been dumb;
And we knew that his spirit was pluming its flight,
That his hour of departure had come.
Still the clock kept the time, with a soft
      and muffled chime,
As we silently stood by his side.

HAIL, HAIL, THE GANG'S ALL HERE

Traditional

HEY DIDDLE DIDDLE

Traditional

HEY, HO! NOBODY HOME

Traditional

HICKORY DICKORY DOCK

Traditional

HOME ON THE RANGE

Lyrics by DR. BREWSTER HIGLEY
Music by DAN KELLY

1. Oh, give me a home where the
2. of-ten at night when the
3.,4. *See additional lyrics*

buf-fa-lo roam, where the deer and the
heav-ens are bright, from the light of the

an-te-lope play, _____ where
glit-ter-ing stars, _____ have I

F   F7   Bb

sel - dom is heard a dis - cour - ag - ing

Bbm   F/C   C7

word, and the skies are not cloud - y all

1-3   F   4   F

day. _____

day. _____

2. How
3. Where the day. _____
4. Oh,

8va

rit. e dim.   ***p***

8vb

Additional Lyrics

3. Where the air is so pure and the zephyrs so free,
And the breezes so balmy and light;
Oh, I would not exchange my home on the range
For the glittering cities so bright.
To Chorus

4. Oh, give me a land where the bright diamond sand
Flows leisurely down with the stream,
Where the graceful white swan glides slowly along,
Like a maid in a heavenly dream.
To Chorus

HOT CROSS BUNS

Traditional

HUMPTY DUMPTY

Traditional

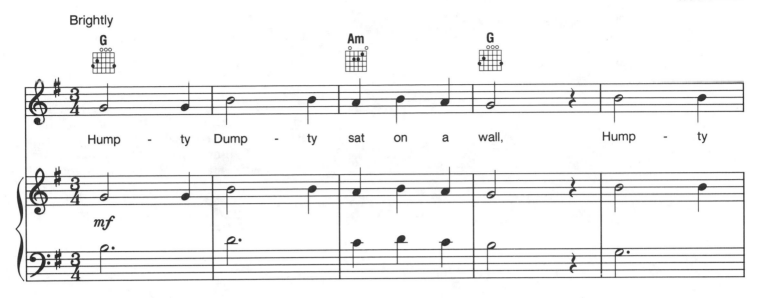

Humpty Dumpty sat on a wall, Humpty

Dumpty had a great fall; All the King's horses and

all the King's men, Could not put Humpty together again.

HUSH, LITTLE BABY

Carolina Folk Lullaby

I'VE BEEN WORKING ON THE RAILROAD

American Folksong

Some-one's in the kit-chen with Di - nah, Some-one's in the kit-chen I know,_____

Some-one's in the kit-chen with Di - nah, Strum-min' on the old ban - jo and sing-in',

"Fee, fi, fid-dle-ee - i - o, Fee, fi fid-dle-ee - i - o,_____

Fee, fi, fid-dle-ee-i - o," Strum-min' on the old ban - jo.

IF YOU'RE HAPPY
AND YOU KNOW IT

Words and Music by
L. SMITH

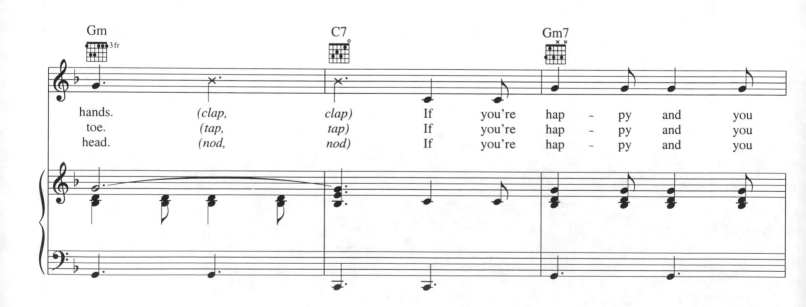

IT'S RAINING, IT'S POURING

Traditional

JACK AND JILL

Traditional

JOHN JACOB JINGLEHEIMER SCHMIDT

Traditional

JESUS LOVES ME

Words by ANNA WARNER
Music by WILLIAM BRADBURY

With Expression

Je - sus loves me! This I know, For the Bi - ble tells me so;
Je - sus loves me! He who died, Heav - en's gate to o - pen wide;

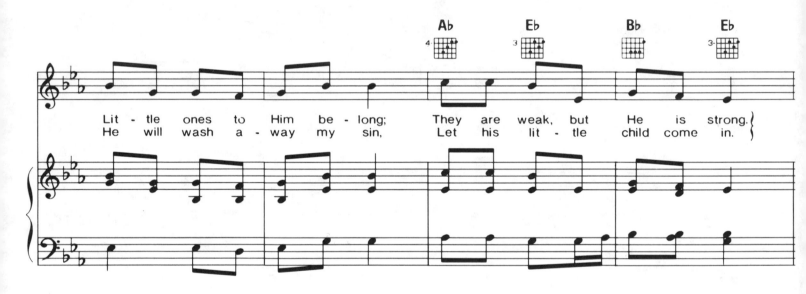

Lit - tle ones to Him be - long; They are weak, but He is strong.
He will wash a - way my sin, Let his lit - tle child come in.

Yes, Je - sus Loves Me! Yes, Je - sus Loves Me! Yes, Je - sus

KUM BA YAH

Traditional

LAVENDER'S BLUE

Traditional

LAZY MARY, WILL YOU GET UP?

Traditional

La-zy Ma-ry, will you get up, will you get up, will
Oh, no, Moth-er, I won't get up, I won't get up, I

you get up? La-zy Ma-ry, will you get up? Will
won't get up. Oh, no, Moth-er, I won't get up, I

you get up to-day? _____
won't get up to-day. _____

LITTLE BO-PEEP

Traditional

LITTLE BOY BLUE

Traditional

LITTLE JACK HORNER

Traditional

Lit-tle Jack Hor-ner sat in a cor-ner, eat-ing a Christ-mas pie. He put in his thumb and pulled out a plum and said, "What a good boy am I!"

LITTLE MISS MUFFET

Traditional

LONDON BRIDGE

Traditional

3. Iron bars will bend and break,
   Bend and break, bend and break;
   Iron bars will bend and break,
   My fair lady.

4. Build it up with gold and silver,
   Gold and silver, gold and silver;
   Build it up with gold and silver,
   My fair lady.

THE MAN ON THE FLYING TRAPEZE

Words by GEORGE LEYBOURNE
Music by ALFRED LEE

Left in the wide world to fret and to mourn, be -
e'er he ap - peared how the hall loud - ly rang with o -
fa - ther, he sighed, and her moth - er, she cried to

trayed by a maid in her teens. _____ Oh, the girl that I
va - tions from all peo - ple there. _____ He'd _ smile from the
see her throw her - self a - way. _____ 'Twas _ all no a -

loved, she was hand - some _____ and I tried all I
bar on the peo - ple be - low and _ one night he
vail she went there ev'ry night and _ threw her bou -

move - ments were grace - ful, all girls he could please, and my love he
does all the work while he takes his ease, and that's what's be -

pur - loined a - way.
come of my

Now, the love.
Her
Her

Additional Lyrics

4. One night as usual I want to her dear home,
   And found there her mother and father alone.
   I asked for my love, and soon 'twas made known,
   To my horror, that she'd run away.
   She packed up her boxes and eloped in the night
   With him, with the greatest of ease.
   From two stories high he had lowered her down
   To the ground on his flying trapeze.

   Chorus

5. Some months after that I went into a hall;
   To my surprise I found there on the wall
   A bill in red letters which did my heart gall,
   That she was appearing with him,
   He'd taught her gymnastics and dressed her in tights
   To help him live at ease.
   He'd made her assume a masculine name,
   And now she goes on the trapeze.

   Chorus

MARY HAD A LITTLE LAMB

Words by SARAH JOSEPHA HALE
Traditional Music

MICHAEL ROW THE BOAT ASHORE

Traditional Folksong

MISTER RABBIT

Traditional

Moderately

Mis - ter Rab - bit, Mis - ter Rab - bit, your
Rab - bit, Mis - ter Rab - bit, your
Rab - bit, Mis - ter Rab - bit, your
Rab - bit, Mis - ter Rab - bit, your

tail's might - y white. Yes, bless
coat's might - y grey. Yes, bless
ears might - y long. Yes, bless
ears might - y thin. Yes, bless

THE MONKEY SONG

Traditional

THE MULBERRY BUSH

Traditional

4. This is the way we scrub the floor, *etc.*
   So early Wednesday morning.

5. This is the way we mend our clothes, *etc.*
   So early Thursday morning.

6. This is the way we sweep the house, *etc.*
   So early Friday morning.

7. This is the way we bake our bread, *etc.*
   So early Saturday morning.

8. This is the way we go to church, *etc.*
   So early Sunday morning.

THE MUFFIN MAN

Traditional

MY BONNIE LIES OVER THE OCEAN

Traditional

OH WHERE, OH WHERE HAS MY LITTLE DOG GONE

Words by SEP. WINNER
Traditional Melody

OATS, PEAS, BEANS AND BARLEY GROW

Traditional

OH! SUSANNA

Words and Music by
STEPHEN C. FOSTER

THE OLD GRAY MARE

Words and Music by
J. WARNER

Oh! The old gray mare, she ain't what she used to be,

ain't what she used to be, Ain't what she used to be, the

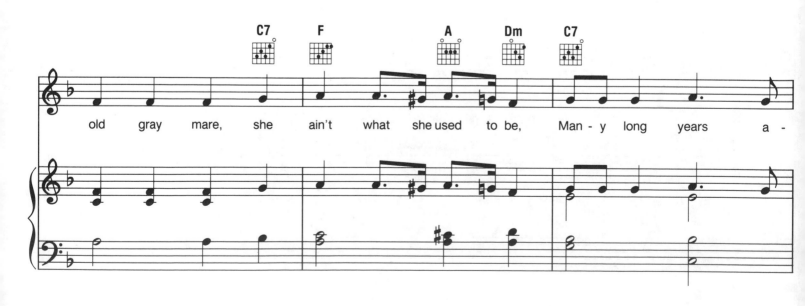

old gray mare, she ain't what she used to be, Man-y long years a-

OLD KING COLE

Traditional

OLD MACDONALD

Traditional Children's Song

1. Old Mac - Don - ald had a farm, E - I - E - I -
2. Old Mac - Don - ald had a farm, E - I - E - I -
3. Old Mac - Don - ald had a farm, E - I - E - I -

O,_____ And on his farm he had a cow, E - I - E - I -
O,_____ And on his farm he had a pig, E - I - E - I -
O,_____ And on his farm he had a duck, E - I - E - I -

4. Old MacDonald had a farm,
   E-I-E-I-O,
   And on his farm he had a horse,
   E-I-E-I-O,
   With a neigh-neigh here and a neigh-neigh there, *etc.*

5. Old MacDonald had a farm,
   E-I-E-I-O,
   And on his farm he had a donkey,
   E-I-E-I-O,
   With a hee-haw here, *etc.*

6. Old MacDonald had a farm,
   E-I-E-I-O,
   And on his farm he had some chickens,
   E-I-E-I-O,
   With a chick-chick here, *etc.*

For additional verses, add your own animals.

ON TOP OF OLD SMOKY

Kentucky Mountain Folksong

court - in' too slow._____ 2. *(see additional lyrics)*

skies._____

2. A-courtin's a pleasure,
   A-flirtin's a grief,
   A false-hearted lover -
   Is worse than a thief.

3. For a thief, he will rob you,
   And take what you have,
   But a false-hearted lover -
   Sends you to your grave.

4. She'll hug you and kiss you,
   And tell you more lies,
   Than the ties on the railroad,
   Or the stars in the skies.

OVER THE RIVER AND THROUGH THE WOODS

Traditional

THE PAW PAW PATCH

Traditional

PEANUT SAT ON A RAILROAD TRACK

Traditional

PEASE PORRIDGE HOT

Traditional

PETER, PETER, PUMPKIN EATER

Traditional

Moderately

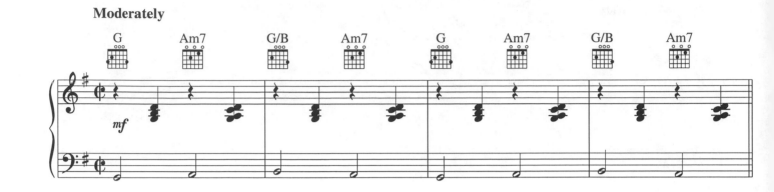

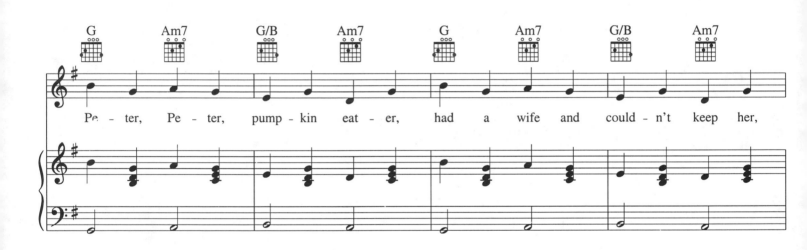

Pe - ter, Pe - ter, pump - kin eat - er, had a wife and could - n't keep her,

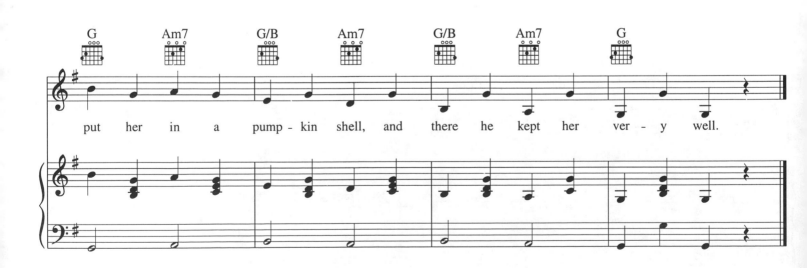

put her in a pump - kin shell, and there he kept her ver - y well.

POLLY PUT THE KETTLE ON

Traditional

POP GOES THE WEASEL

Traditional

RING AROUND THE ROSIE

Traditional

ROCK-A-BYE, BABY

Traditional

SIMPLE SIMON

Traditional

ROW, ROW, ROW YOUR BOAT

Traditional

Mer - ri - ly, mer - ri - ly, mer - ri - ly, mer - ri - ly, Life is but a dream.

A SUGGESTED ACTIVITY

"Row, Row, Row Your Boat" is a famous "round" that has been sung and enjoyed by people of all ages. When sung correctly, the melody actually goes around and around. Here's how it works: The singers are divided into two groups. The first group sings the first line alone. At this point, the second group starts at the beginning, while the first group continues with the second line. In this manner, the groups are always exactly one line apart as the tune is repeated. The last time through, the second group sings the final line alone just as the first group sang the opening line alone. Try it . . . it's fun!

SHE'LL BE COMIN' 'ROUND THE MOUNTAIN

Traditional

3. Oh, we'll all go to meet her when she comes,
   Oh, we'll all go to meet her when she comes,
   Oh, we'll all go to meet her,
   Oh, we'll all go to meet her,
   Oh, we'll all go to meet her when she comes.

4. We'll be singin' ''Hallelujah'' when she comes,
   We'll be singin' ''Hallelujah'' when she comes,
   We'll be singin' ''Hallelujah,''
   We'll be singin' ''Hallelujah,''
   We'll be singin' ''Hallelujah'' when she comes.

SHOO FLY, DON'T BOTHER ME

Words by BILLY REEVES
Music by FRANK CAMPBELL

SIMPLE GIFTS

Traditional Shaker Hymn

'Tis a gift to be sim-ple, 'tis a gift to be free, 'tis a gift to come down where you ought to be, and when we find our-selves in the

SKIP TO MY LOU

Traditional

2. I'll find another one, prettier than you,
   I'll find another one, prettier than you,
   I'll find another one, prettier than you,
   Skip to my Lou, my darling.

3. Little red wagon, painted blue.

4. Can't get a red bird, a blue bird'll do.

5. Cows in the meadow, moo, moo, moo.

6. Flies in the buttermilk, shoo, shoo, shoo.

SWEET BETSY FROM PIKE

American Folksong

Moderately

1. Oh, don't you re-mem-ber sweet
2.-8. *See additional lyrics*

Bet - sy from Pike, who crossed the big moun-tains with her lov - er Ike; with

two yoke of cat - tle, a large yel - low dog, a ___ tall Shang-hai roos - ter, and

Additional Lyrics

2. One evening quite early they camped on the Platte,
   'Twas near by the road on a green shady flat,
   Where Betsy, sore-footed, lay down to repose —
   With wonder Ike gazed on that Pike County rose.
   To Chorus

3. Their wagon broke down with a terrible crash,
   And out on the prairie rolled all kinds of trash,
   A few little baby clothes done up with care,
   'Twas rather suspicious, but all on the square.
   To Chorus

4. The Shanghai ran off, and their cattle all died;
   That morning the last piece of bacon was fried;
   Poor Ike was discouraged and Betsy got mad,
   The dog drooped his tail and looked wondrously sad.
   To Chorus

5. They soon reached the desert where Betsy gave out,
   And down in the sand she lay rolling about;
   While Ike, half distracted, looked on with surprise,
   Saying, "Betsy, get up, you'll get sand in your eyes."
   To Chorus

6. Sweet Betsy got up in a great deal of pain,
   Declared she'd go back to Pike County again;
   But Ike gave a sigh, and they fondly embraced,
   And they travelled along with his arm 'round her waist.
   To Chorus

7. They suddenly stopped on a very high hill,
   With wonder looked down upon old Placerville;
   Ike sighed when he said, and he cast his eyes down,
   "Sweet Betsy, my darling, we've got to Hangtown."
   To Chorus

8. Long Ike and sweet Betsy attended a dance;
   Ike wore a pair of his Pike County pants;
   Sweet Betsy was dressed up in ribbons and rings;
   Says Ike, "You're an angel, but where are your wings?"
   To Chorus

TAKE ME OUT TO THE BALL GAME

Words by JACK NORWORTH
Music by ALBERT VON TILZER

Take me out to the ball game

Take me out to the crowd. _____

THERE WAS AN OLD WOMAN WHO LIVED IN A SHOE

Traditional

There _ was an old wom-an who lived in a shoe. She had so man-y

chil-dren, she did-n't know what to do. She _ gave them some broth with -

out an-y bread. She _ whipped them all sound-ly and put them to bed.

THERE'S A HOLE IN THE BOTTOM OF THE SEA

Traditional

158

frog on the bump on the log in the hole in the bot-tom of the

sea. There's an eye, there's an

eye, there's an eye on this flea, there's a

flea on the wing, there's a wing on the fly, there's a

THERE'S A HOLE IN THE BUCKET

Traditional

Additional Lyrics

3. With what shall I fix it, dear Liza, etc.
4. With a straw, dear Henry, etc.
5. But the straw is too long, dear Liza, etc.
6. Then cut it, dear Henry, etc.
7. With what shall I cut it, dear Liza, etc.
8. With a knife, dear Henry, etc.
9. But the knife is too dull, dear Liza, etc.
10. Then sharpen it, dear Liza, etc.

11. With what shall I sharpen it, dear Liza, etc.
12. With a stone, dear Henry, etc.
13. But the stone is too dry, dear Liza, etc.
14. Then wet it, dear Henry, etc.
15. With what shall I wet it, dear Liza, etc.
16. With water, dear Henry, etc.
17. In what shall I carry it, dear Liza, etc.
18. In a bucket, dear Henry, etc.

19. There's a hole in the bucket, dear Liza, etc.

THIS LITTLE LIGHT OF MINE

African-American Spiritual

THIS OLD MAN

Traditional

With spirit

This old man, he plays *one, He plays nick-nack *on my drum, With a

nick, nack, pad-dy whack, give a dog a bone, This old man came roll-ing home. roll-ing home.

*Two . . . . on the shoe
*Three . . . on the tree
*Four . . . . on the door
*Five . . . . on the hive
*Six . . . . . on the sticks
*Seven . . . up in heaven
*Eight . . . on the gate
*Nine . . . . on the line
*Ten . . . . . once again

THREE BLIND MICE

Traditional

Brightly

Three blind mice, Three blind mice,

See how they run, See how they run! They

all run af-ter the farm-er's wife; She cut off their tails with a

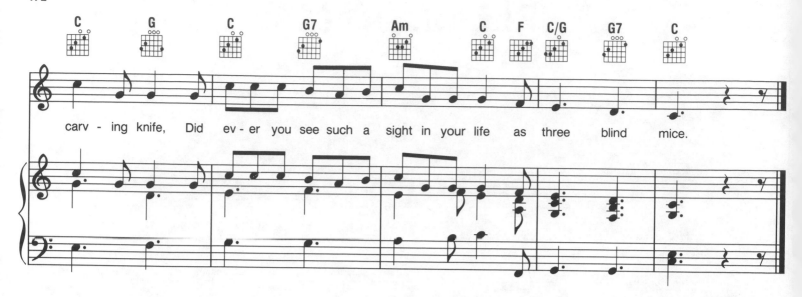

carv - ing knife, Did ev - er you see such a sight in your life as three blind mice.

YANKEE DOODLE

Traditional

With spirit

1. Yan - kee Doo - dle went to town A - rid - ing on a
2. Fath'r and I went down to camp A - long with Cap - tain
3. There was Cap - tain Wash - ing - ton Up - on a slap - ping

po - ny,   Stuck a feath - er in his cap And
Good - win.   There we saw the men and boys As
stal - lion,   Giv - ing or - ders to his men;   I

THREE LITTLE KITTENS

Traditional

Moderately

Once three lit - tle kit - tens they lost their mit - tens, and
The three lit - tle kit - tens they found their mit - tens, and
The three lit - tle kit - tens put on their mit - tens, and

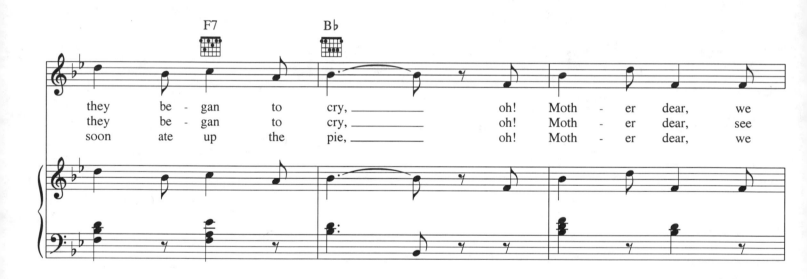

they be - gan to cry, _____ oh! Moth - er dear, we
they be - gan to cry, _____ oh! Moth - er dear, see
soon ate up the pie, _____ oh! Moth - er dear, we

sad - ly fear, our mit - tens we have lost. _____ What,
here, see here, our mit - tens we have found. _____ What,
great - ly fear, our mit - tens we have soil'd. _____ What,

TWINKLE, TWINKLE LITTLE STAR

Traditional

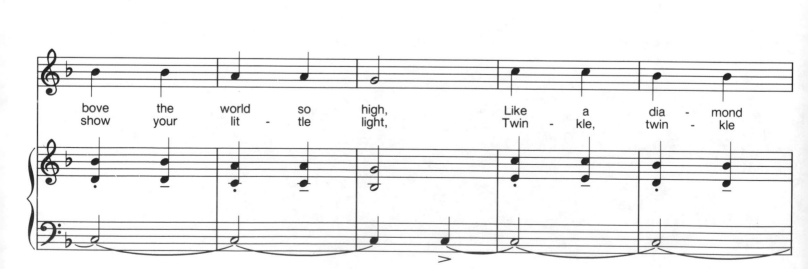

Parody

Starkle, starkle, little twink,
How I wonder what you think!
Up above the world so high,
Think you own the whole darn sky?
Starkle, starkle, little twink,
You're not so great,
That's what I think!

WHEN THE SAINTS GO MARCHING IN

Words by KATHERINE E. PURVIS
Music by JAMES M. BLACK

Bb + Eb + Ab.

YOU'RE A GRAND OLD FLAG

Words and Music by
GEORGE M. COHAN

ZACCHAEUS WAS A
WEE LITTLE MAN

Traditional

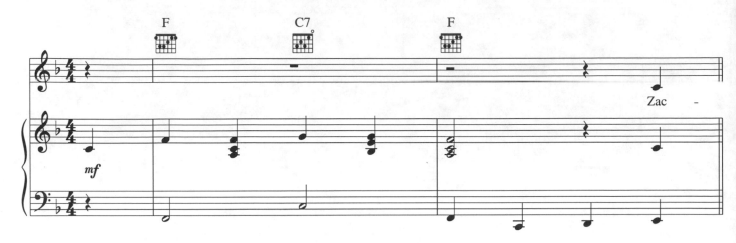

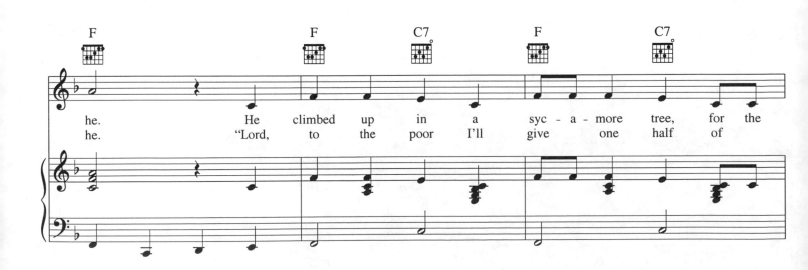

TOM, TOM, THE PIPER'S SON

Traditional